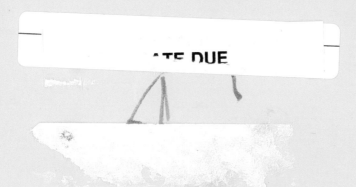

DATE DUE

BUGS

NANCY WINSLOW PARKER
AND
JOAN RICHARDS WRIGHT

Illustrations by Nancy Winslow Parker

Greenwillow Books, New York

NOTE

The scientific symbols for male, ♂ , and female, ♀ , are used throughout the text. The line ⊢——⊣ denotes the actual size of the bug. The three types of insecta metamorphosis— simple, incomplete, and complete—are indicated as $\boxed{S}$, $\boxed{I}$, and $\boxed{C}$.

In the labeling of the enlarged bugs, the plural has been used for antenna (pl., antennae), palpus (pl., palpi), and tarsus (pl., tarsi).

A black pen line was combined with watercolor paints and colored pencils for the full-color art.
The typefaces are Sabon and Symbol.

Printed in U.S.A. First Edition 10 9 8 7 6 5 4 3

Library of Congress Cataloging-in-Publication Data Parker, Nancy Winslow. Bugs.
Bibliography: p. 40 Summary: Includes general information, jokes, and brief descriptions of the physical characteristics, habits, and natural environment of a variety of common insects. 1. Insects—Juvenile literature. [1. Insects] I. Wright, Joan Richards. II. Title. QL467.2.P35 1987 595.7 86-29387
ISBN 0-688-06623-2 ISBN 0-688-06624-0 (lib. bdg.)

To Amanda, Emily, Jimmy, and Peter
J. R. W.

and to Clyde (*Felis domestica*) and Carrie
N. W. P.

Grateful acknowledgment is made to Mr. Louis Sorkin, M.S.,
R.P.E., the Department of Entomology, The American
Museum of Natural History, for checking the scientific
accuracy of the drawings and text, and to Ms. Frances Lesser,
B.S., M.L.S., the Library of the Academy of Natural
Sciences of Philadelphia.

What bug bit Thelma on the thigh?

A horsefly.

HORSEFLY

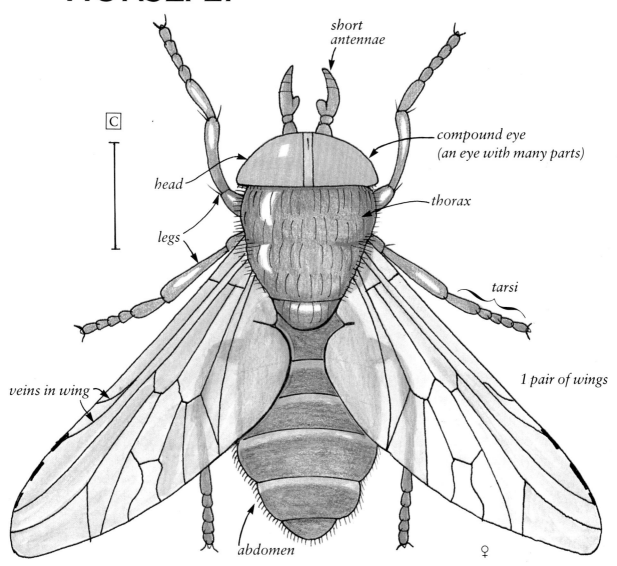

short antennae

compound eye
(an eye with many parts)

C

head

thorax

legs

tarsi

veins in wing

1 pair of wings

abdomen

♀

AMERICAN HORSEFLY *(Tabanus americanus)*

A hard-biting horsefly nipped Thelma. Horseflies live and breed near swamps
and stagnant water. The male horsefly feeds on pollen and nectar, the female
on blood. The female's bite bleeds longer than other insects' bites because her
saliva contains a chemical that prevents blood clotting. The American Horsefly
is found on the Atlantic seaboard and in the midwest from Texas to Canada's
Northwest Territories. Flies are everywhere.

Whose shrill sound woke Ada?

A cicada.

CICADA (sick-ada)

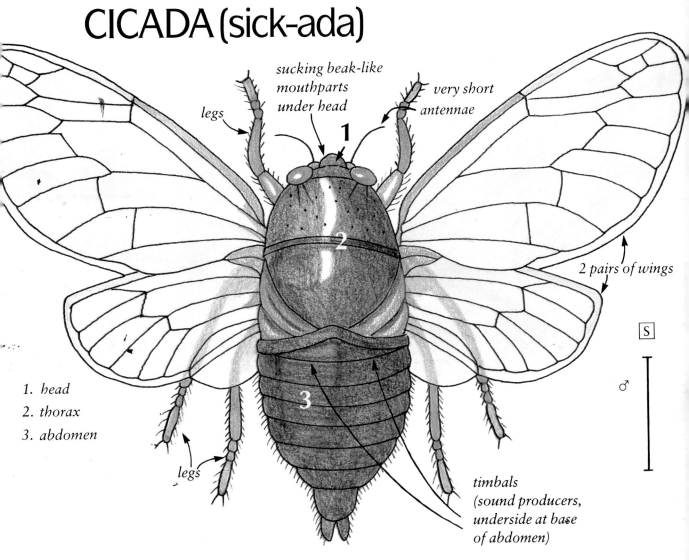

sucking beak-like mouthparts under head

very short antennae

legs

1

2

2 pairs of wings

S

♂

legs

3

timbals (sound producers, underside at base of abdomen)

1. *head*
2. *thorax*
3. *abdomen*

PERIODICAL CICADA (*Magicicada septendecim*)

A cicada's loud buzzing sound woke Ada. Cicadas are found in and near woods. The Periodical Cicada takes 17 years (northern, eastern, and western varieties) or 13 years (southern variety) to grow from egg to nymph to adult. The female damages twigs and branches when she lays her eggs on them. During late summer, when cicadas hatch, one can see thousands of empty nymph skins attached to trees and bushes. The newly-emerged adults, who will live for only 4–6 weeks, do not eat. Only male cicadas make sounds. Periodical Cicadas are found in the eastern and central United States. Other species are found over much of the United States.

What crawled into Grant's shirt and pants?

Ants.

ANT

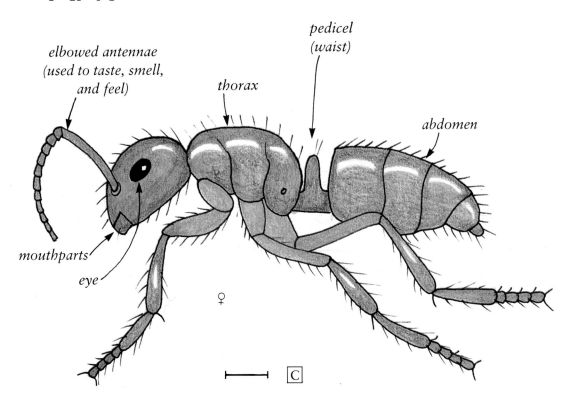

elbowed antennae
(used to taste, smell,
and feel)

pedicel
(waist)

thorax

abdomen

mouthparts

eye

♀

C

BLACK CARPENTER ANT (*Camponotus pennsylvanicus*)

Grant foolishly sat on a rotten log at the picnic. It was full of Black Carpenter
Ants. Unlike termites, ants do not eat wood, but only chew tunnels and
galleries so they can live in the decaying wood. Ants live in large groups called
colonies and have various jobs. The queen lays eggs, and workers excavate
tunnels, gather food, and care for the nest. Some colonies have soldiers who
defend the colony. Most ants eat other insects. Ants found in the kitchen are
either the sweet-eating (sugar) or grease-eating (bacon) variety. Ants are black,
brown, reddish-, or brownish-yellow in color. They live in deserts, woods,
trees, and sand, under stones, at high elevations, in open fields, in houses and
gardens, in grass, and in clay. The Black Carpenter Ant is found along the east
coast and in the central United States. In general, ants are found all over the
United States.

What bug made
Nick's dog sick?

A tick.

TICK

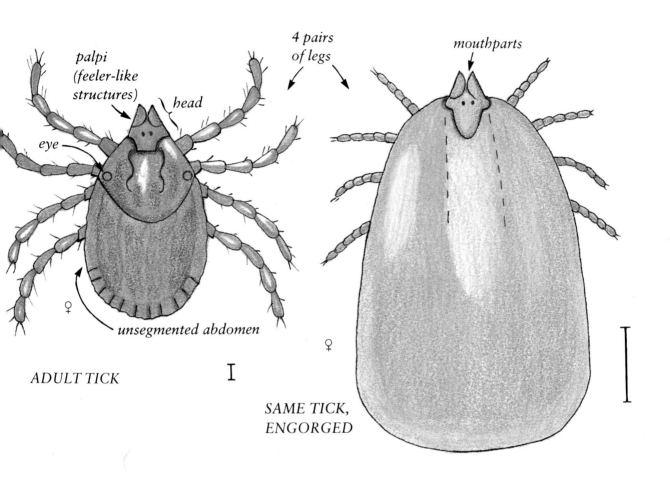

palpi
(feeler-like
structures)

head

eye

4 pairs
of legs

mouthparts

♀

unsegmented abdomen

ADULT TICK

SAME TICK,
ENGORGED

♀

BROWN DOG TICK (*Rhipicephalus sanguineus*)

A Brown Dog Tick is clinging to the dog's ear. The dog's blood provides food for the tick. The tick attaches itself to the dog with anchor-like mouthparts as the dog walks through fields, woods, or parks. Other species of tick attack cattle, sheep, horses, chickens, and people. Some ticks spread disease, so check pets and clothing after a walk in the countryside. Ask your veterinarian how to remove a tick safely. Don't just yank it off! The Brown Dog Tick is found east of the Mississippi River, although other species are found in many other places.

What jumped from
Queenie's back when
she was squeezed?

Fleas.

FLEA

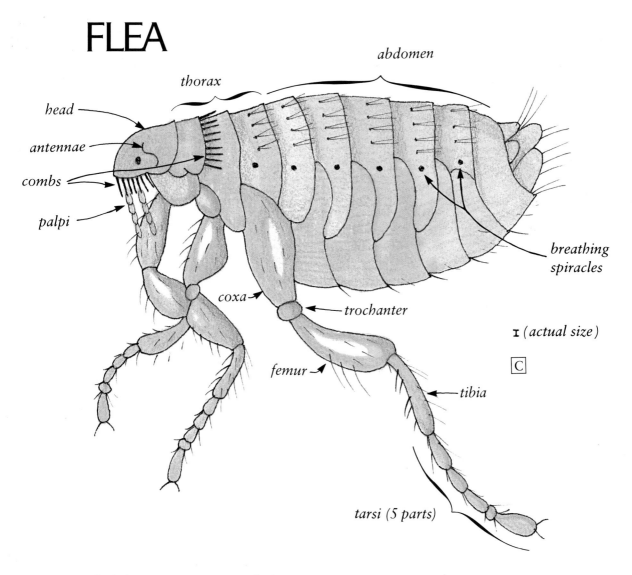

thorax

abdomen

head

antennae

combs

palpi

breathing
spiracles

coxa

trochanter

femur

tibia

ɪ *(actual size)*

C

tarsi *(5 parts)*

CAT FLEA *(Ctenocephalides felis)*

The tiny fleas that jumped off Queenie are found on cats and dogs. The female Cat Flea lays her eggs in the cat's bedding or hair. The larvae eat dried skin and dirt near the cat's bed. The adult flea feeds on the cat's blood. Fleas are found on pigs, rats, mules, deer, birds, and people. They also find their way into vacuum cleaners and rugs. Fleas are extremely flat. They look as if they were ironed out or stepped on. Their narrow bodies make it easy for them to move through an animal's hair. Some fleas spread disease. Fleas are among the insect world's greatest jumpers. The extra long hind legs have enlarged coxae, which help them leap a foot or more. Fleas are found all over the world.

What slippery bug
made Doug say "ugh"?

A slug.

SLUG

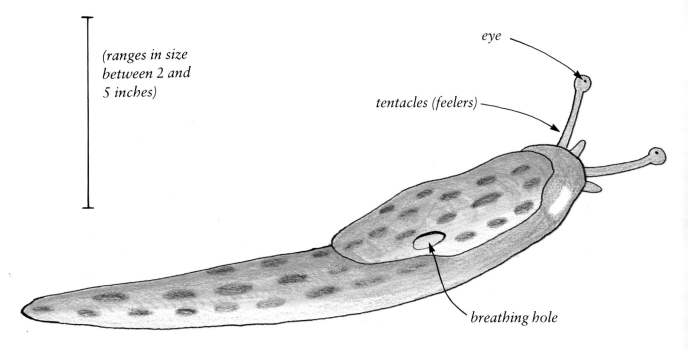

(ranges in size between 2 and 5 inches)

eye

tentacles (feelers)

breathing hole

SPOTTED GARDEN SLUG (Limax maximus)

The soft brown creature that Baby Doug saw on the flower petal was a slug, which looks like a snail without a shell. The slug lives in damp, dark places that help keep its skin from drying out. After a thunderstorm or shower or at night, the slow-moving slugs come out of their hiding places in the garden. As they move along, they leave slimy trails on plants, paths, and buildings. Most slugs eat only leaves and plants. The clammy, foul-tasting coat most slugs have is one defense against their enemies, although some insects, such as fireflies, are slug-eaters. Some slugs bite. The good thing about slugs is that they enrich the soil by helping to break up plant matter; the bad thing is that they are garden pests. Slugs are found all over the world. The Spotted Garden Slug, once found only in Europe, is now found all over the United States.

What did Sam find swimming in his apple cider?

A spider.

SPIDER

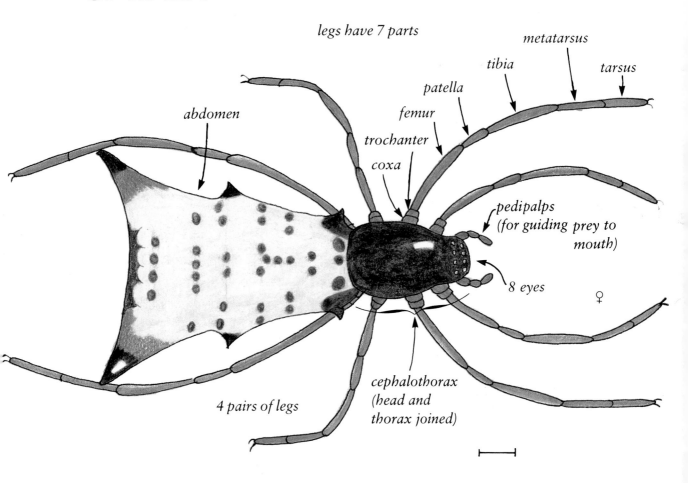

legs have 7 parts

metatarsus

tibia

tarsus

patella

femur

trochanter

coxa

abdomen

pedipalps
(for guiding prey to mouth)

8 eyes

♀

cephalothorax
(head and thorax joined)

4 pairs of legs

ARROW-SHAPED MICRATHENA *(Micrathena sagittata)*

The unlucky spider that fell into Sam's drink was probably an Arrow-shaped Micrathena, a small spider that sits in its web with its belly up and its head tilted down, and weaves a web with a hole in the middle. In the fall, the female lays her eggs on a leaf near her web. Her pointy spines make her an unattractive meal for hungry birds. The Arrow-shaped Micrathena is found in woods and fields, spinning the web that helps it catch its insect prey. The venom in a spider's fangs paralyzes or kills its victim, which the spider then eats. The Arrow-shaped Micrathena is found throughout the United States. There are 35,000 other spider species. Not all spiders spin webs. Spiders are found all over the world.

What bug fell into
Ben's broth?

A moth.

MOTH

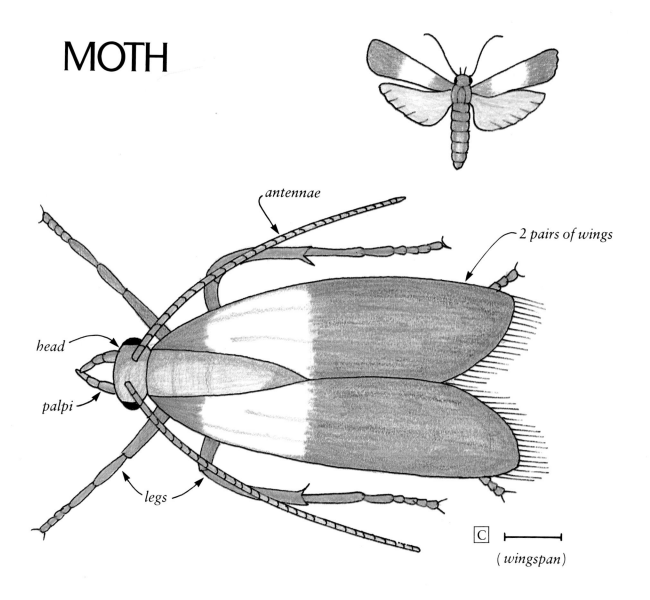

antennae

2 pairs of wings

head

palpi

legs

C ⊢———⊣

(*wingspan*)

INDIAN MEAL MOTH (*Plodia interpunctella*)

It was probably an Indian Meal Moth that found its way out of the pantry and into Ben's broth. Indian Meal Moths are often found in homes and other places where food is stored; they eat various kinds of human food, especially grains, cereal, beans, crackers, and cookies. The female lays 300-400 eggs which hatch, grow into caterpillars, and then become adults within a few months. These moths are considered pests and are difficult to control. Moths are found all over the world, on trees and screened porches, and in forests, yards, parks, orchards, and closets.

What left a bump when
it bit Rita?

A mosquito.

MOSQUITO

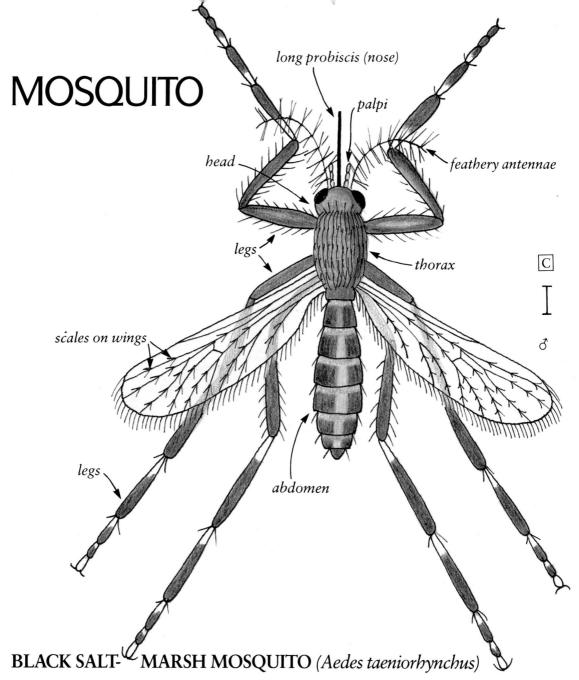

long probiscis (nose)

palpi

head

feathery antennae

legs

thorax

C

scales on wings

♂

legs

abdomen

BLACK SALT- MARSH MOSQUITO *(Aedes taeniorhynchus)*

Even out rowing on the bay, Rita was bitten by a Black Salt-marsh Mosquito. The males do not bite, but feed on plant nectar. The females bite and feed on blood. Strong fliers, mosquitoes travel many miles from their breeding grounds. Mosquitoes are a vacationer's most annoying bug, biting constantly and ruining outdoor fun. Even worse, some species carry diseases such as yellow fever and malaria. There are 2,500 species of mosquito, and they are found almost everywhere. The Black Salt-marsh Mosquito is found on the Atlantic coast, along the Gulf coast, and in southern California.

What ran across the rug full speed?

A centipede.

CENTIPEDE

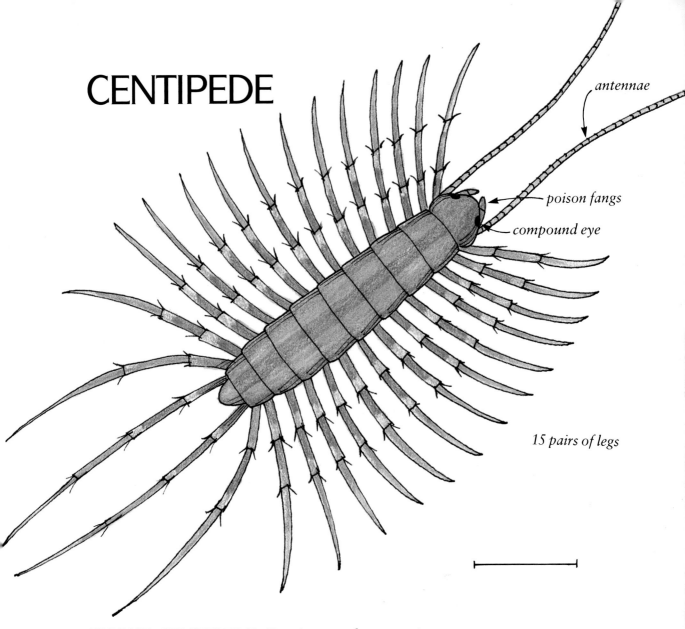

antennae

poison fangs

compound eye

15 pairs of legs

HOUSE CENTIPEDE *(Scutigera coleoptrata)*

The centipede that ran across Grandma's rug might have been a House Centipede. Centipedes are found inside houses, running along floors and walls at astonishing speeds. They live outdoors in warmer climates. The House Centipede is born with only 7 pairs of legs, but the number increases to 15 as it grows. Centipedes like dark places and can be found under stones, under houses, in cracks, and in leaf mold. Most centipedes are not dangerous, but the poison released from even a small centipede's bite can cause pain. The House Centipede is found throughout the United States, but about 3,000 known species of centipede are found all over the world.

What ran over Grandma's brooch?

A roach.

ROACH

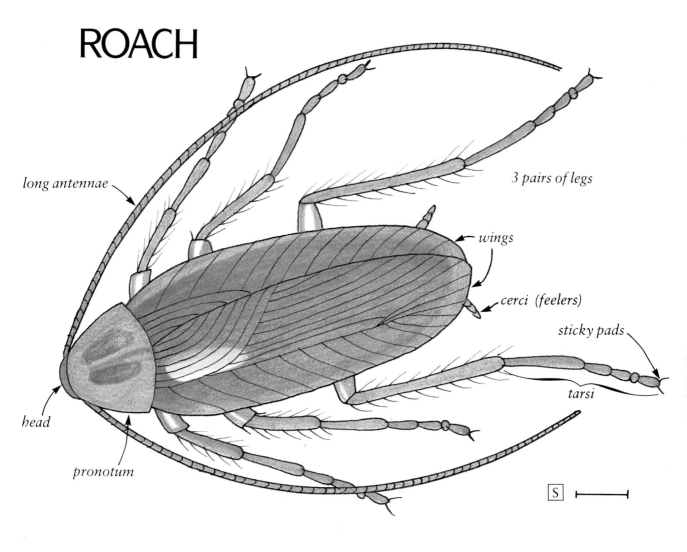

long antennae

3 pairs of legs

wings

cerci (feelers)

sticky pads

tarsi

head

pronotum

S

GERMAN COCKROACH (Blatella germanica)

A German Cockroach ran across Grandma's brooch. Cockroaches eat almost anything people eat, coming out at night to look for food. Some cockroaches can climb straight up on smooth surfaces because of the sticky pads on their legs. The female lays her eggs in well-hidden places, which makes it difficult to find and kill them. Cockroaches can spread disease. There are 3,500 species of cockroach, 60 of which are found in North America. Cockroaches are among the world's oldest insects; scientists have found fossils that tell us they lived millions of years ago. The German Cockroach and other species of this bug live all over the world in homes, stores, restaurants, and ships.

What chirped as Nick
walked through the thicket?

A cricket.

CRICKET

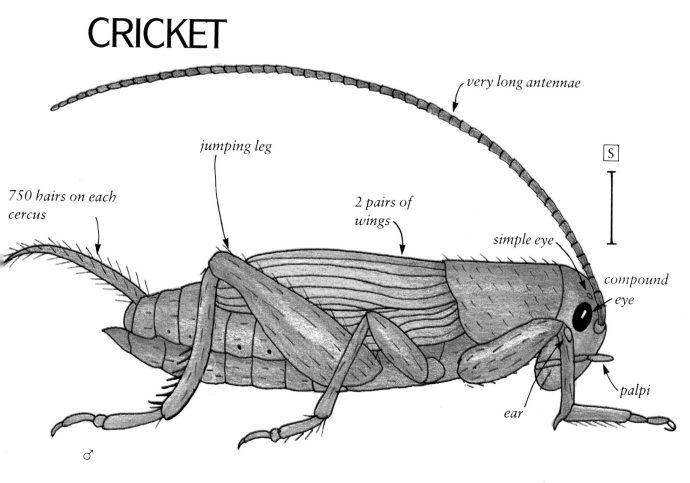

very long antennae

jumping leg

750 hairs on each cercus

2 pairs of wings

simple eye

compound eye

palpi

ear

♂

S

FIELD CRICKET (*Gryllus pennsylvanicus*)

The Field Cricket that Nick heard lives in the undergrowth of fields and woods. It eats both plants and other insects. When the weather turns cold, some crickets come inside to keep warm. Crickets live in caves, houses, fields, trees, and underground. Some crickets damage crops and eat flowers; some eat blankets and sweaters. Male crickets make chirping sounds by rubbing their wings together. That is the way they communicate with other crickets. The Field Cricket, the House Cricket, and the Tree Cricket rarely stop chirping. The rate of the cricket's chirping varies with the air temperature. The Field Cricket is found throughout the United States. Various species of crickets are found all over the world.

TERMITES

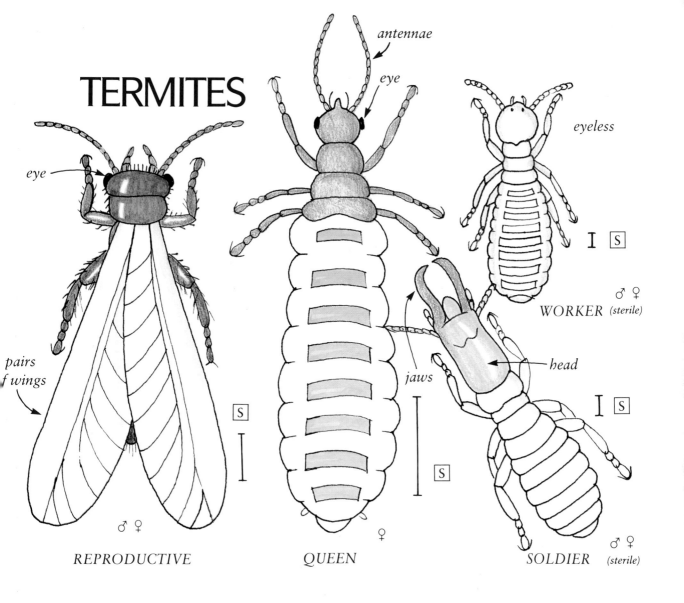

antennae

eye

eye

eyeless

I S

WORKER (sterile) ♂ ♀

pairs of wings

jaws

head

S

S

I S

♂ ♀

REPRODUCTIVE

♀

QUEEN

SOLDIER (sterile) ♂ ♀

EASTERN SUBTERRANEAN TERMITE *(Reticulitermes flavipes)*

The porch collapsed because tiny creatures called Eastern Subterranean Termites had eaten the wooden supports. Tiny organisms called protozoans live in the termite's stomach and help it digest the wood. Termites live in damp wood, where they make tunnels and galleries to house a very complicated social system: a queen who lays eggs, reproductive termites who can also produce eggs if something happens to the queen, a bevy of workers who care for the young and the queen, and soldiers who defend the entire colony. Porches, furniture, trees, houses, and barns sometimes collapse because of these destructive bugs. The Eastern Subterranean Termite is found on the eastern seaboard and as far west as the Mississippi River. Termites are a worldwide pest.

What bug did the nurse see on Ada's blouse?

A louse.

LOUSE

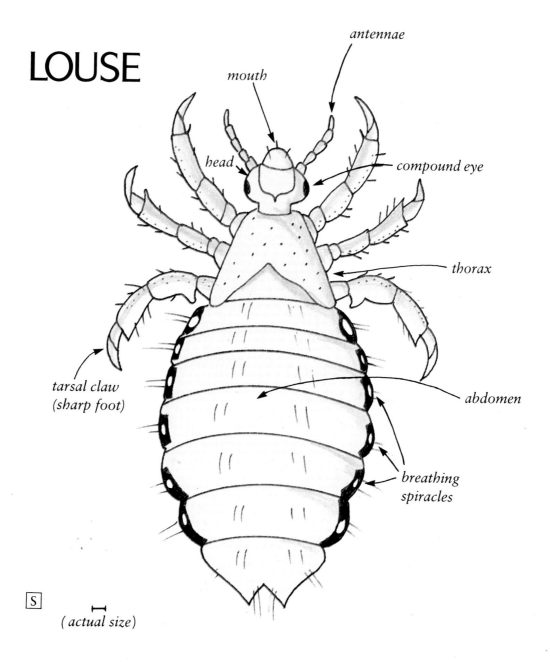

antennae

mouth

head

compound eye

thorax

tarsal claw
(sharp foot)

abdomen

breathing
spiracles

S

(actual size)

HEAD LOUSE *(Pediculus humanus capitis)*

The tiny wingless bug that the nurse spotted on Ada's blouse was a louse. The Head Louse is found on human heads. It is parasitic, and needs a host animal in order to survive. The Head Louse feeds on blood. Lice spread from person to person. Some lice carry disease. Frequent bathing, and washing of bed linen and clothing usually keep lice away. Lice are found all over the world. Hogs, sheep, horses, and even penguins at the South Pole have lice.

What twinkled its light
in the twilight sky?

A firefly.

FIREFLY

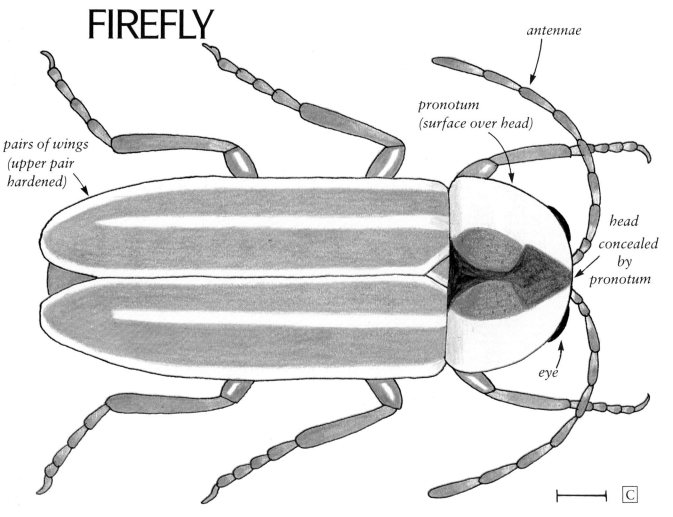

antennae

*pronotum
(surface over head)*

*pairs of wings
(upper pair
hardened)*

*head
concealed
by
pronotum*

eye

C

PENNSYLVANIA FIREFLY *(Photuris pennsylvanicus)*

Rita and Ada like to catch fireflies at dusk in the summer. Fireflies, also called lightning bugs, are found in fields, woods, and backyards. The larvae live under bark or wet leaves and eat soft insects, worms, and snails. But the male Pennsylvania Firefly, in its adult stage, which lasts about two weeks, does not seem to eat at all. The female sometimes eats other fireflies. Fireflies come out at night and blink to attract a mate. Pennsylvania Fireflies blink every few seconds while flying. A chemical reaction in the firefly causes its abdomen to light up. The firefly's larva, called a glowworm, is also luminous. Fireflies are found all over the United States. The Pennsylvania Firefly is found on the east coast, in the central states, and in the midwest.

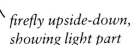

*firefly upside-down,
showing light part*

What fluttered its wings
as it flew by?

A dragonfly.

DRAGONFLY

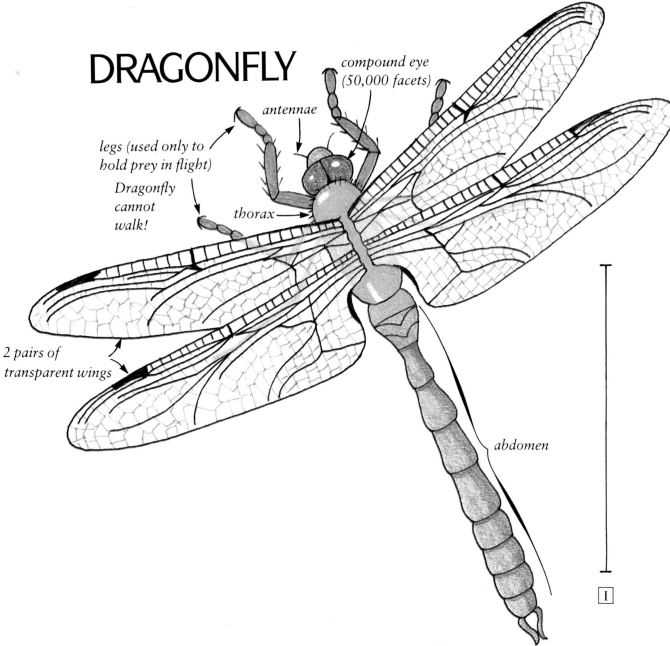

compound eye (50,000 facets)

antennae

legs (used only to hold prey in flight)
Dragonfly cannot walk!

thorax

2 pairs of transparent wings

abdomen

I

GREEN DARNER *(Anax junius)*

The children spotted a Green Darner, or Darning Needle, as it flew by at the beach. Green Darners are among the largest and fastest of the dragonflies. The young dragonfly begins life in the water as a naiad where it feeds on tiny fish and insects. The dragonfly's long legs are not used for walking, but to hold the insects that it captures while flying. As adults, dragonflies benefit man by gobbling up thousands of mosquitoes. Green Darners and other dragonflies live in marshes near rivers and ponds all over North America.

How Bugs Grow

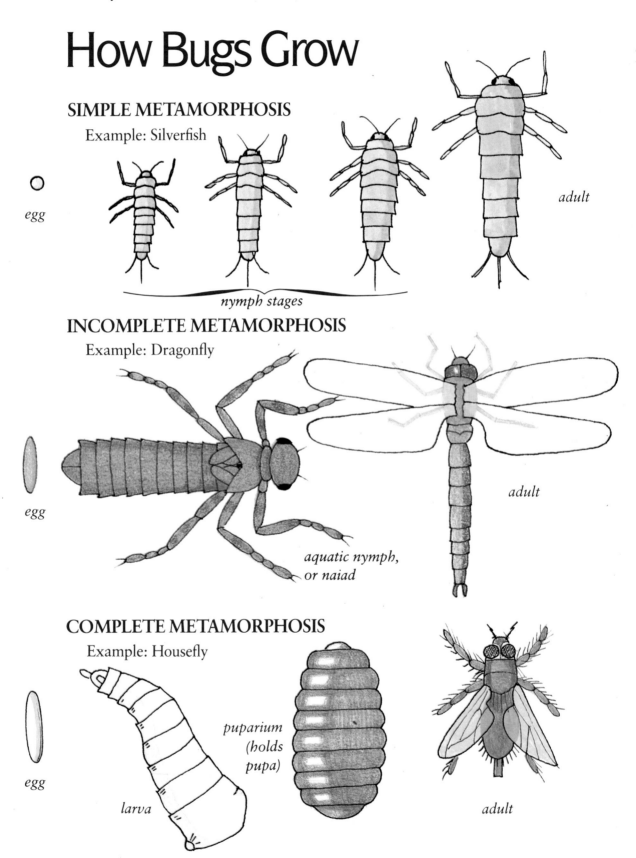

SIMPLE METAMORPHOSIS

Example: Silverfish

egg

nymph stages

adult

INCOMPLETE METAMORPHOSIS

Example: Dragonfly

egg

aquatic nymph, or naiad

adult

COMPLETE METAMORPHOSIS

Example: Housefly

egg

larva

puparium (holds pupa)

adult

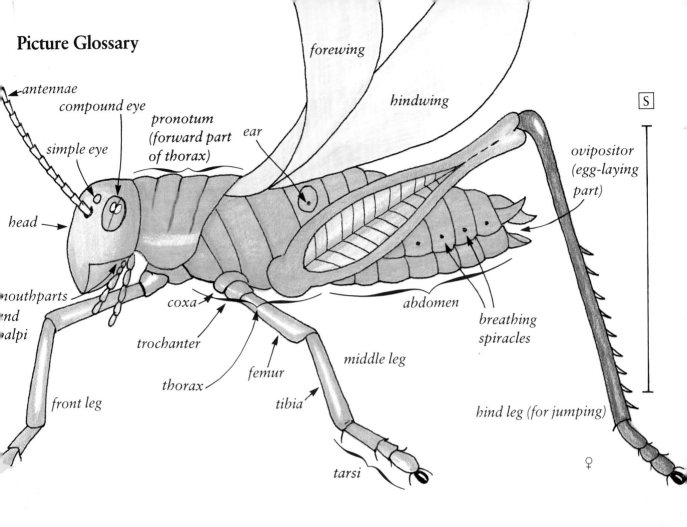

antennae
compound eye
simple eye
pronotum
(forward part
of thorax)
ear
forewing
hindwing
S
ovipositor
(egg-laying
part)
head
mouthparts
and
palpi
coxa
trochanter
thorax
femur
front leg
middle leg
tibia
abdomen
breathing
spiracles
tarsi
hind leg (for jumping)
♀

Example of a Typical Bug

The grasshopper is a typical bug or insect. Like all adult insects, the grasshopper has:

1. a body with three parts: thorax, head, and abdomen
2. a thorax with 1 or 2 pairs of wings, and 3 pairs of legs
3. legs, which are always in 5 sections
4. a head with antennae, eyes, and mouthparts
5. mouthparts for biting, sucking, piercing, sipping, or lapping.

Other bug cousins, such as spiders, ticks, and centipedes, have slightly
different bodies from insects, but retain the joint-legs of their common phylum.

Examples of Growth Stages

THE EGG AND EGG CASE

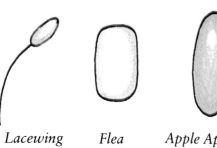

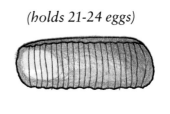

(holds 21-24 eggs)

Lacewing   Flea   Apple Aphid   German Cockroach egg case   Citrus Red Mite

LARVA

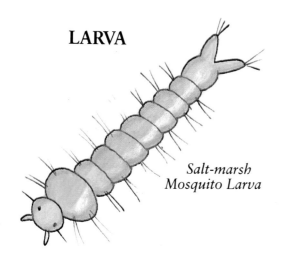

Salt-marsh Mosquito Larva

Larvae of some flies are MAGGOTS

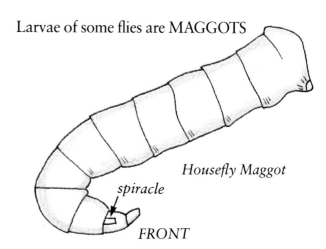

Housefly Maggot

spiracle

FRONT

Larvae of beetles are GRUBS

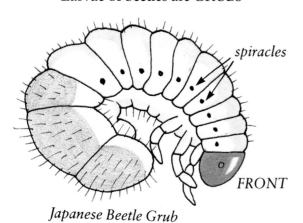

spiracles

FRONT

Japanese Beetle Grub

Larvae of butterflies and moths are CATERPILLARS

Banded Woollybear
Larva of Isabella Tiger Moth

Picture Glossary

NYMPH—looks like adult, only smaller

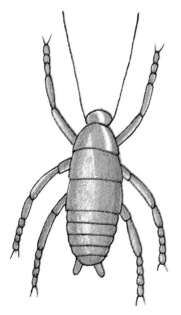

Cockroach Nymph

NAIAD—The early growth of some insects takes place in water. At that stage, the insect is called a naiad or aquatic nymph.

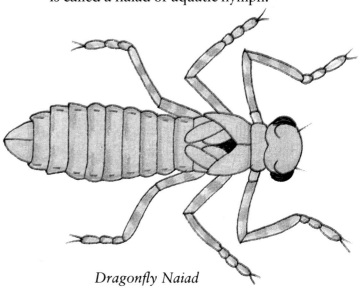

Dragonfly Naiad

PUPA—middle stage of growing insect or bug

Apple Maggot

COCOON—a case made of silken threads that holds the growing insect

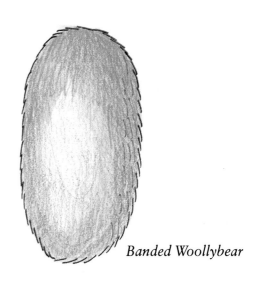

Banded Woollybear

KINGDOM: ANIMAL

PHYLUM: ARTHROPODA (Joint-legged)

Class	Order	Example	Mouthtype	Wings (adult)
Insecta	Diptera	Fly, mosquito	Piercing-sucking	1 pair
Insecta	Homoptera	Cicada	Piercing-sucking	2 pairs
Insecta	Hymenoptera	Ants	Biting-chewing	2 pairs (reproductives)
Insecta	Siphonaptera	Fleas	Piercing-sucking	none
Insecta	Lepidoptera	Moth	Siphoning	2 pairs
Insecta	Orthoptera	Cricket	Biting-chewing	2 pairs
Insecta	Dictyoptera	Roach	Biting-chewing	2 pairs
Insecta	Isoptera	Termites	Biting-chewing	2 pairs (reproductives)
Insecta	Anoplura	Lice	Sucking	none
Insecta	Coleoptera	Firefly	Biting-chewing	2 pairs
Insecta	Odonata	Dragonfly	Biting-chewing	2 pairs
Chilopoda	Scutigeromorpha	Centipede	Chewing with poison claws	none
Arachnida	Acarina	Tick	Sucking	none
Arachnida	Araneae	Spider	Biting	none

PHYLUM: MOLLUSCA

Gastropoda	Zonitacea	Slug	Scraping	none

Bibliography

Arnett, Ross H., Jr., and Richard L. Jacques. *Simon and Schuster's Guide to Insects.* New York: Simon and Schuster, 1981.

Borror, Donald J., and Richard E. White. *A Field Guide to the Insects of America North of Mexico.* The Peterson Field Guide Series, edited by Roger Tory Peterson. Vol. 19. Boston: Houghton Mifflin, 1970.

Burton, Maurice, and Robert Burton. *Encyclopedia of Insects and Arachnids.* London: Octopus Books, 1975.

Callahan, Philip S. *Insects and How They Function.* New York: Holiday House, 1971.

Evans, Glyn. *The Life of Beetles.* New York: Hafner Press, Macmillan Publishing Co., 1975.

Evans, Howard Ensign. *Life on a Little Known Planet.* New York: Dutton, 1968.

Gertsch, Willis John. *American Spiders.* 2nd ed. New York: Van Nostrand Reinhold, 1979.

Graham, Ada, and Frank Graham. *Busy Bugs.* New York: Dodd, Mead, 1983.

Green, Ivan E., and G. A. Smith. *Hatch and Grow: Life Stories of Familiar Insects Shown in Close-up Photographs by George A. Smith.* London: Abelard-Schuman, 1967.

Grzimek, Bernhard. *Grzimek's Animal Life Encyclopedia.* Vols. I, II, III. New York: Van Nostrand Reinhold, 1972.

Jacobson, Morris K., and David R. Franz. *Wonders of Snails and Slugs.* New York: Dodd, Mead, 1980.

Levi, Herbert W., and Lorna R. Levi. *Spiders and Their Kin.* New York: Golden Press, 1968.

Milne, Lorus J., and Margery Milne. *The Audubon Society Field Guide to North American Insects and Spiders.* New York: Knopf, 1980.

Swan, Lester A., and Charles S. Papp. *The Common Insects of North America.* Foreword by Evert I. Schlinger. New York: Harper & Row, 1972.

Tweedie, Michael. *Atlas of Insects.* New York: John Day, 1974.